MEN AT
CHURCH

MEN AT
CHURCH

DON SHIRK

Regular Baptist Press
1300 North Meacham Road
Schaumburg, Illinois 60173-4806

DEDICATION

To my dad, Richard J. Shirk.
You modeled the art of a faithful life and
what this book is all about.

MEN AT CHURCH
© 2003
Regular Baptist Press • Schaumburg, Illinois
1-800-727-4440
www.regularbaptistpress.org
Printed in U.S.A.
RBP5300 • ISBN:1-59402-029-9

CONTENTS

PREFACE

I love working with men. There is nothing like the distinct cama-
raderie that comes with men interacting with men. Whether it is on
the playing field, in the workplace, or in the great outdoors, men with
men forge special bonds. But one area where men play a significant
role with one another has been greatly neglected: church. The challenge of writing lessons on the subject *Men at Church* is that it con-
veys all the excitement of a big yawn while you watch your grass
grow.

While it is vital for men to know the doctrine of the church, un-
derstood in theological terms as the doctrine of ecclesiology, that is
not what this book is about. This book considers the Biblical teaching
of what men at church are to *be*. It investigates how men who profess
to know Christ should learn and grow and what real manhood looks
like—both inside and outside the four walls of your local church.
Consequently, *Men at Church* sets forth a distinctive challenge for
men who are serious about authentic manhood in the only institution
Jesus Christ ever established.

Enjoy the journey.

1

MEN AT CHURCH . . .

KNOW HOW TO BEHAVE

This study will help you understand the significance of your role as a man at church.

MEN AT CHURCH are a rare breed. For years the statistics of our culture prove that, for the most part, it was "women at church": women teaching Sunday School, women at prayer meeting, women serving, women in charge and men in tow. Mark it down: God loves women, and women play a vital role in church life, but a look at the bulk of Biblical evidence points to a whole lot more male church activity than what exists in many churches today. Somewhere along the line we lost that legacy.

Until now. That's why *you* are working through this book. You *want* to be a God-made man. Perhaps you never thought of it, but God has divinely created you to be male. The bottom line? Guys are naturally drawn to guy stuff. Also, the fact that you currently are in some sort of "church" setting (such as an adult Sunday School class or Bible study) says that in some way, shape, or form, church is special to you and the things of God interest you. The bottom line? Church stuff is guy stuff. Sure, women are an essential part of God's program in His church. But men dedicated to God are to accept and assume their God-designed place in His church. Thus, the purpose of the following lessons is to demonstrate the truth that "men at church" are the living reality of what Christ continues to build (Matthew 16:18). They are not a mirage, but are *real* men.

"This Isn't Your Father's Oldsmobile!"

Remember the commercial that pronounced, "This isn't your father's Oldsmobile"? What was it saying? Besides trying to get you to buy a new car, it was saying that the times and culture had drastically changed. And now Oldsmobiles aren't even being built! Each new generation brings drastic changes.

Consider these facts about the students who will enter college in the fall of 2004, most of whom were born in 1982:

- We have always been able to reproduce DNA in the laboratory.
- We have always been able to receive television signals by direct broadcast satellite.
- There have always been ATM machines.
- Around-the-clock coverage of congress, public affairs, weather reports, and rock videos have always been available on cable.
- They have never heard a phone "ring."
- Congress has been questioning computer intrusion into individuals' personal lives since they were born.
- "Spam" and "cookies" are not necessarily foods.[1]

These facts demonstrate the changes in technology from one generation to the next. However, technology isn't the only thing that has drastically changed. Even the very way we live has changed. Not only is the "traditional" family the exception today, but so is the traditional "church-going" family. For many men coming into the church from unchurched backgrounds, church life is about as familiar as Mars. They lack a basic grasp of the Biblical components that comprise a genuine local New Testament church. So let's begin with getting a handle on some needed basics about men at church.

"Men . . ."

1. How has the face of manhood changed from what it was twenty-five years ago? fifty years ago? _____

   _____

   _____

   _____

2. What has contributed to this change?_____

   _____

   _____

   _____

". . . at . . ."

3. Think of and list the various places we men spend time.

   • _____

   • _____

   • _____

   • _____

   • _____

   • _____

   • _____

   • _____

4. What do these observations reveal about our lives? _____

_____

_____

_____

5. What do they reflect about our priorities? _____

_____

_____

_____

6. What guidance do Psalm 90:12 and Romans 13:11 and 12 provide concerning the places where we spend our time?

_____

_____

_____

". . . Church"

7. What is unique about church? _____

_____

_____

Note the following Biblical truths about your church:
- It is central to God's program today (Matthew 16:18).
- God is building it (Matthew 16:18).
- It is a place of hope and victory (Matthew 16:18).
- Believers in the New Testament joined and actively participated in it (Acts 2:41, 42).
- Men are equipped at church to accomplish God's priorities for life (Ephesians 4:12–16).
- Both belief and conduct matter there (1 Timothy 3:15; 1 Corinthians 3:11–17).

Unraveling the Mystery

So just what is it that men at church are to do? While many New Testament books teach truth about the local church, this study will focus primarily on three small but powerful books: 1 Timothy, 2 Timothy, and Titus. Commonly called the Pastoral Epistles, they are not for clergy only! Rather, these books offer a unique glimpse into real manhood in the setting of the local church.

Written by the apostle Paul, these books provide a look into the heart of a man's man interacting with men. Paul possessed the needed balance of being both tough and tender. The Lord used Paul's consecrated character to mentor both Timothy and Titus in the practical outworking of local church life.

Look up the following passages to discover Paul's balance of toughness and tenderness: 1 Timothy 1:20; Titus 3:10; 1 Timothy 5:3; 2 Timothy 4:11.

8. How do we men at church need this balance in our character?

_____

_____

Behavior Basics

So why did Paul write these books? First Timothy 3:15 provides the answer: "That thou mayest know how thou oughtest to behave thyself in the house of God, which is the church of the living God, the pillar and ground of the truth." (Read 1 Timothy 3:14–16.)

Needed: responsible men

In verse 15 the little word "that" reveals Paul's purpose in writing: to strengthen Timothy in his personal responsibilities in leading the church. Paul encouraged Timothy to step up to the plate and assume the responsibility of leadership entrusted to him.

9. It is interesting to observe how many men shy away from respon-

sibility, not only at church, but in everyday areas as well. Why do men have this tendency? _____

_____

_____

10. What do we need to do to counter this tendency? _____

_____

_____

Needed: knowledgeable men

Verse 15 reads, "That thou mayest know." Paul knew that much of Timothy's survival would depend on his knowing certain truths. This particular word "know" refers to the possession of knowledge or skill necessary to accomplish a desired goal. Paul was not speaking of mere intellectual knowledge but of hands-on knowledge of what to do in given situations in the church.

11. What do men need to know to have a working knowledge of the local church? _____

_____

12. How does the local church benefit when men are equipped with this understanding? _____

_____

Needed: consistent men

First Timothy 3:15 says, in part, "that thou mayest know how thou oughtest to behave thyself in the house of God." The word "behave" describes more than simple behavior, such as passing out bulletins or picking up empty communion cups. Rather it speaks of a consistent pattern of life. Local churches need men who are dependable and faithful, not up one week and down the next, here one week and gone for three, on fire for the Lord this month and in spiritual Antarctica the next.

13. How can we develop a consistent pattern of life that honors God?

_____

_____

14. In what areas do we men need a consistent pattern of life?

_____

_____

15. List the benefits to your church when men are consistent in their walk with the Lord.

- _____
- _____
- _____
- _____
- _____
- _____

Needed: church-going men

One of the well-known hymns of the faith is "Take My Life and Let It Be"; it has been rewritten by some to read, "Take my wife and let her be Consecrated, Lord, to Thee; Take my children as Thine own; As for me, I'll stay at home!" Strong, knowledgeable, and consistent men do two things when it comes to church.

First, they do not avoid church. Demonstrating their commitment and leading their families, they show that the things of the Lord have priority; consequently, they are "in the house of God." When the doors are open, they are there. They do not take lightly circumstances that squeeze them out of the house of God. Rather than letting good things, such as sports and community activities, dictate their calendar, they allow the things of the Lord to take priority. Times when they might have to miss church because of a conflict are the exception rather than the rule.

Second, when they are in church, they conduct themselves properly because they grasp three critical truths.

Truth 1: They know Who's in charge. The local church is "the church of the living God" (1 Timothy 3:15). It belongs to Him. He, not the men, owns it.

16. What can happen in a church when men think it is "their" church? _____

_____

Truth 2: They know what's at stake. It is "the church of the living God, the pillar and ground of the truth" (1 Timothy 3:15). "Truth" refers to the divine revelation of the gospel and the content of the Christian faith.

17. Why is truth so important in church? _____

_____

_____

_____

Truth 3: They know Who to follow.

18. First Timothy 3:16 presents six descriptions of Jesus Christ. How do these descriptions reveal the worthiness of Christ and our need to follow Him exclusively? _____

_____

_____

_____

_____

Nothing is more exciting than men at church discovering the joy of worshiping and serving the living God! Pray that this spiritual journey will shape you (through your behavior and character) into a useful, godly man at church.

1. "Class of 2004 Mindset," Beloit College, http://www.beloit.edu/~pubaff/mindset/2004.html

2

MEN AT CHURCH . . .

READ THE DIRECTIONS

This study will help you see the importance of having a Bible-centered life.

WHY DO MEN never stop to ask for directions? Because they aren't lost; they just don't know where they are! Men and directions . . . always good fodder for jokes. Whether they are taking a vacation trip or assembling toys at Christmas, men and directions seem to be at odds.

1. What are directions?_____

_____

_____

2. Why do men have this negative reputation with directions?

_____

_____

The Direction Dilemma

Interestingly, our tension is with written directions, isn't it? Think about it: you have to stop what you are doing to read a map; you have to stop what you are doing to read the assembly directions to put that widget with wheels together. So we often conclude, "Why bother with directions? I can figure it out myself!"

3. Think through the following reasons for our resistance with directions. What is it about each of them that can cause us frustration?

When it comes to directions . . .
• You have to stop.
• You have to read.
• You have to be patient.
• You have to submit to a person or plan other than yourself.
• You have to follow.
• You have to admit you might not know where you are going or what you are doing.
• Other: _____

Righting Our Wrong Direction

My twenty-year-old daughter needed directions to drive to a friend's house five hours away. I was mentally occupied with a variety of issues and was listening with half an ear as she retraced her route to make sure she was correct. At one point she said, "And then I go west." To which I responded, "Right." But I was wrong. She needed to go east. It was a two-hour mistake in the wrong direction. As her father, I felt terrible. I had given my daughter wrong directions.

Right from the get-go men are headed in the wrong direction. Psalm 58:3 teaches that men go "astray as soon as they [are] born." Consequently, "There is a way which seemeth right unto a man, but the end thereof are the ways of death" (Proverbs 14:12).

Spiritually, we are lost in sin. As a consequence of choosing our own way, life is hard (Proverbs 13:15). However, the great news is that God, through His Son, has not only provided salvation from sin but has also delivered us from our bent to go in the wrong direction! The tools He has graced us with to rescue us from our own way are His powerful presence in the person of the Holy Spirit and His guiding Word: "Thy word is a lamp unto my feet, and a light unto my path" (Psalm 119:105). God's directions are fully trustworthy because they are without error!

Second Timothy 3:16 teaches us about the accurate and authoritative nature of the Bible: "All scripture is given by inspiration of God, and is profitable." Therefore, men at church can look to it with confidence and live by it wholeheartedly, because they know it will never lead them in the wrong direction.

Note the following facts about why the Bible is profitable:
- It teaches us what is right: "doctrine."
- It teaches us what is wrong: "reproof."
- It teaches us how to right the wrong: "correction."
- It teaches us how to keep it right: "for instruction in righteousness."

4. Read 2 Timothy 3:17. What are the results that men will see in their lives as they receive and apply the directions of the Bible?

_____

_____

An Age-Old Issue

The Pastoral Epistles expose the fact that our modern penchant toward directional dysfunction did not begin with Henry Ford and the invention of the automobile. When it comes to cars, "Ford has a better idea!" However, when it comes to the church, no one has any better ideas than God. His directions for what the church is to believe and how it is to function are nonnegotiable. Yet, even though God has provided an infallible resource in the Bible, church history is filled with examples of men who thought they could "improve on" the clear direction of God's revealed will.

5. Look up the following passages of Paul's instructions to Timothy and Titus. Note the kinds of difficulties they were having with men not following God's directions at church. Think about whether or not these issues continue to exhibit themselves in churches today, and if so, how.

- 1 Timothy 1:3, 4: Men who thought their way was better.

- 1 Timothy 1:6, 7: Men who in ignorance confidently gave wrong directions.

- 1 Timothy 1:18–20: Men who threw away the directions.

- 1 Timothy 4:1–5: Men who were not bothered that their directions were wrong.

- 1 Timothy 6:1–6; Titus 2:9, 10: Men who hurt the testimony of Christ because they couldn't handle directions in the workplace.

- 2 Timothy 2:14, 16–18: Men who did not grasp the danger of wrong directions.

6. In Titus 1:10–16 and 3:9–11 Paul gave strong counsel to Titus in the "why and how-to" of dealing with men who insist on giving wrong direction at church. List some character traits of these men, according to these verses. _____

_____

_____

_____

7. Describe the negative results of the wrong directions these men gave. _____

_____

8. Discuss the course of action Paul set forth in dealing with this kind of problem. _____

_____

_____

The Joke Stops Here

Real men at church take God's directions seriously. Not only do they follow them, but they seek to have their lives molded by them. They understand the authoritative nature of the Bible, so they work at becoming more familiar with it than with the *TV Guide*. Not only that, but men at church make sure the Scriptures are "front and center" in everything that occurs at church. In a culture that maximizes entertainment and minimizes the work of worship, they realize that for their lives and church life to go in the right direction, both must be permeated with the Bible.

9. Read 1 Timothy 4:13. List the three components of a Biblically saturated way of life to which Timothy was to continually give his attention.

  • _____

  • _____

  • _____

10. Why are each one of these important, and how will they give direction to men at church? _____

_____

_____

_____

_____

_____

Why Men at Church Read and Obey God's Directions

The Pastoral Epistles are filled with examples of how the Bible's directions are to shape and influence men at church. When men are serious about learning and growing, they know that only God's directions matter (1 Timothy 1:3). They know the value of what God's directions produce (1 Timothy 1:5), and they want to avoid dire consequences by staying on the track of godly living (1 Timothy 1:18–20; 6:20, 21). They desire the safety of spiritual character that comes only through obedience to the Bible (1 Timothy 6:11–14).

11. From 2 Timothy 2:2 what do we discover men are to do with the Biblical directions they have learned in God's Word?

_____

_____

12. What are some creative ways this can take place between men at church?

- _____

- _____

- _____

13. Titus 1:3 teaches that God has "manifested his word through preaching." What are some thoughtful ways men can encourage their pastor in his responsibility to faithfully preach God's directions?

- _____

- _____

- _____

Leaving a Legacy

It is a treasured keepsake: a photo on Christmas Day with me and my plastic "Gung-Ho!" army helmet looking over the shoulder of my dad, who was pouring over the assembly directions to a huge toy crane rig. That picture is more than a memory. It captures my father's attitude toward directions. You see, I did not grow up with an "anti-direction" dad. Anytime we got a new something as a family or I made a purchase, it was *always*, "Read the directions first." In 1974 Dad bought a new VW Super Beetle. Cool car. And I was a more-than-willing driver. The prerequisite to driving it? Read the owner's manual.

The interesting thing about my dad was that his "obsession" with directions did not stop with material things. It was a way of life that went with him to church and left with him after church. My dad was a quiet man, so for me he was E. F. Hutton: when he spoke, I listened. A familiar sight in our home was Dad sitting in his chair with Bible in hand, having his devotions or preparing to teach his men's Sunday School class. One time while he was doing this, I asked him a question—to this day I cannot remember the question, but I never forgot his answer. He said, "Don, read the book of Proverbs and pray for wisdom." That advice deeply penetrated my heart and set the course of my life.

Dad also followed the directions at church. How do I know? As a family, we were faithful to all the services at church. He served at church from A to Z. He supported the pastor and weathered the storms of false accusation and rough business meetings. He would be the first to admit that he wasn't perfect, but for me his example of reading God's directions for living gave me needed direction for life.

14. The busyness of our lives is one of the difficulties hindering many men in spending time in God's Word. What are some things we can do that will help us take the time to stop and read God's directions?

• _____

- _____
- _____
- _____

15. What do we need to be doing now if we want to leave a positive legacy of humble submission and obedience to God's Word in our lives?

- _____
- _____
- _____

During the war in Iraq, an American maintenance convoy made a wrong turn that resulted in the tragic loss of lives as the soldiers found themselves surrounded by the enemy. Perhaps you have experienced some extreme difficulties because of wrong turns. Pray that you would have a renewed desire to follow God's directions—not only to get you back on track but also to keep you on track in living for Him!

3

MEN AT CHURCH . . .

GRASP GRACE

This lesson will encourage you to grasp the true understanding of grace.

THE STORY IS told of a prince who ventured into the galley of a slave ship. As he walked around, he asked the prisoners why they were there. "I should not be here. I'm innocent!" said many. "I've been falsely accused!" cried others. The prince walked through the entire ship, hearing excuse after excuse. Finally he came upon one man who, when asked why he was there, replied, "I have every right to be here. I am guilty of the crime I committed and am deserving of my punishment." The prince responded, "It's a pity such a bad fellow like you should be here with all these innocent people; I think I'll set you free!"

Grace. Men who grasp it are men who remember well the bondage from which they've been undeservedly set free.

Grace Basics

In Scripture the basic thought behind the word "grace" is "free giving." It means "to show favor or kindness, to give as a favor, to be gracious to someone, to pardon." It portrays the process by which an owner turns and graciously gives what he has to someone in need. Many times grace is needed because of offense and guilt. Interestingly, the word comes from a word that means "joy," or "that which delights." So what is grace? Grace is God's giving us what we do not deserve. It results in genuine joy!

Amazing Grace

"Amazing grace—How sweet the sound—That saved a wretch like me!" We know the tune, but do we know its truth?

More than any other apostle, Paul focused on the truth of grace. He was a man who never got over it, because he unmistakably experienced its life-changing effect. Much of his writing is personalized instruction about the awesome truths of grace in action.

1. R. T. Forsyth said, "Our churches are full of the nicest, kindest people who have never known the despair of guilt or the breathless wonder of forgiveness." Do you agree with this statement? Why or why not? _____

_____

Men at church are not there to network with other businessmen or to "look good" as people of the community. They are there because of one overarching reason: God's grace has changed their lives.

Read 1 Timothy 1:12–17 and note the benchmarks of the man who grasps grace.

• He has a past: "who was before" (1 Timothy 1:13). While we do not enjoy hanging out all our dirty laundry, a genuine testimony is able to say, "Here's what my life was like *before* I was saved."

• He has an honest admission of guilt: "who was before a blasphemer, and a persecutor, and injurious" (v. 13). Most men at church will not have a one-for-one match between their past behavior and Paul's, but what they will have is genuine honesty about their guilt as sinners.

• He has a defining moment: "but I obtained mercy" (v. 13). Men at church came to a point in time, a spiritual defining moment, in which they were "born again" (John 3:3) and became new creatures in Christ (2 Corinthians 5:17).

• He has true relief: "I obtained mercy" (v. 13). While grace is God's giving us what we do not deserve, mercy is His sparing us from what we *do* deserve. In the experience of God's mercy, the "despair of guilt" is replaced with "the breathless wonder of forgiveness."

• He never gets over grace: "and the grace of our Lord was exceeding abundant" (v. 14). Paul put it another way in Romans 5:20 when he exclaimed, "But where sin abounded, grace did much more abound." Whether you were saved at age five or fifty, if you understand your sinfulness and have a true grasp of grace, you never get over the humbling question, "Why did God save *me?*"

• He centers his life on the person and work of Jesus Christ: "this is a faithful saying, and worthy of all acceptation, that Christ Jesus came into the world to save sinners; of whom I am chief" (v. 15). Men at church minimize their story and maximize His story!

• He strives to be a positive testimony for Christ (especially in difficult times): "Howbeit for this cause I obtained mercy, that in me first Jesus Christ might shew forth all longsuffering, for a pattern to them which should hereafter believe on him to life everlasting" (v. 16). Men who know firsthand the rescue of grace want, in turn, to be rescuers!

• He praises the awesome character of God: "Now unto the King eternal, immortal, invisible, the only wise God, be honour and glory for ever and ever. Amen" (v. 17).

Turning Up the Magnification:
Needed Questions about Amazing Grace

Review the following questions about your grasp of grace.

• Do you have a "past," or is your "present" more like your past?

• Have you ever honestly admitted your guilt as a sinner? Could pride be your worst enemy?

• Have you had a defining moment in your spiritual journey, a time when you were born again? Maybe you cannot remember the exact date, but *when* was that time?

• Do you have true relief because you know you were spared from what you deserve?

• Is the recollection of your salvation experience matter-of-fact and routine, or do you still stand in awe of God's work of salvation in your life?

• Is Jesus Christ the one person you trust for your salvation? Is He the one you live for because of Who He is and what He did for you, or is your life marked by trying to fit in and be a somebody at church?

• Are you burdened for someone who is in as desperate need of being rescued from sin as you were? Who is that person?

• Do you regularly praise God for Who He is and what He is doing in your life?

How Sweet the Sound!

Grace is more than a single-stringed instrument. Not only does it affect our salvation, but it also produces a variety of other beautiful spiritual results as we learn and grow as believers. God gives us a new, purposeful agenda!

2. What are some of the things that men live for every week?

_____

_____

_____

3. Second Timothy 1:9 teaches that God has "saved us . . . according to his own purpose and grace." For what purposes did Christ save us men at church—purposes that are now to be priorities in our lives?

_____

_____

_____

4. Second Timothy 2:1 encourages us to "be strong in the grace that is in Christ Jesus." The context of this verse deals with working with all kinds of people in the church. Describe the ways grace will strengthen you in working with various people at church.

_____

_____

_____

_____

Tuition-Free Grace!

I have five children. Two are presently in college; a third will soon be; and the other two are not far behind. I understand something of the cost of higher education! Sometimes the cost of obtaining a college education can put that achievement out of reach. Such is never the case in God's school of grace!

Titus 2:11–13 is a classic passage on the education that grace gives the believer. Grace not only saves us, but it also actively teaches us.

5. Read Titus 2:11–13. What two things are we to deny, according to verse 12?

- _____

- _____

6. Bill is a deacon and is active in a variety of ministries at church. He is also a businessman who travels out of town at least once a month. What no one knows is that Bill struggles with viewing pornography while he's alone in his motel room. Upon coming home after each trip, he is smitten with guilt and vows never to do it again. But the next time he's away, the temptation is too great, and he does it again. In his frustration and brokenness he comes to *you* for help. What do you tell him?

_____

_____

_____

_____

_____

7. In what three positive ways does grace instruct us to counter ungodliness and worldly lusts (Titus 2:12)?

• We are to live _____ .

• We are to live _____ .

• We are to live _____ .

8. What do each one of these points mean? _____

_____

_____

_____

9. What will men who model these truths be like at church?

_____

_____

_____

10. How would these aspects of a godly life help Bill in his situation?

_____

_____

Grace is more than just a word. It is more than a theological concept. It is an unmistakable encounter with the eternal and incomprehensible, loving initiative of God.

Simply put, when God's grace finds a man and does its work, that man knows it. Do you know you are saved? Pray that your spiritual journey will be marked by a growing grasp of grace!

4

MEN AT CHURCH ...

GROW

This study will demonstrate the
truth that when grace happens,
growth occurs.

I AM NOT A farmer, but I do enjoy keeping a little garden. There is something about working with the ground, planting, and seeing things grow. Several years ago I planted a few apricot trees and now enjoy bumper crops of beautiful, golden fresh apricots, even in the snowbelt of western New York!

1. What needs to be present for things to grow?

_____

_____

2. What occurs in growth?

_____

_____

3. Men at church *grow*. What does this statement imply?

_____

_____

Avoiding Pumpkin-Patch Theology

One summer a small patch of pumpkin plants thrived in my garden. Having never grown them before, I was fascinated at how large the leaves became and how well they sheltered what went on underneath them. If you wanted to see the evidence of what was going on, you really needed to poke around!

Often our Christian culture portrays spirituality as something "personal" and "private." Like those pumpkin plants, we shelter our lives against any kind of accountability and sense of responsibility to "examine yourselves, whether [you are] in the faith" (2 Corinthians 13:5). Jesus cursed a fig tree that looked good from a distance but that, upon close examination, offered only leaves (Mark 11:12–14). When it came to spiritual fruit, Paul—like Jesus—was passionate about men evidencing genuine spiritual growth and fruit as its result.

Does this situation sound familiar? John has been a church member for twenty years. In business meetings he is "front and center" in debating matters at hand, yet he refuses to pray either in small gatherings on Wednesday night or if asked to pray before a church service.

4. When a man can be very vocal in one area, like business meetings, and very quiet in other areas, like prayer meetings, what possible dynamics are going on? _____

_____

Spiritual Showtime 101

We're not talking about being a spiritual show-off. Such behavior is clearly condemned throughout the Bible, especially by Jesus (Matthew 6:1–5). In 1 Timothy 4:11–16 Paul exhorted Timothy with a series of ten present-tense commands about the critical need for *observable* spiritual growth in three areas: character (v. 12), Bible knowledge (v. 13), and spiritual giftedness (v. 14). In verse 15 Paul encouraged, "Meditate upon these things," or give careful thought to, the spiritual truths he was teaching.

5. What everyday items and issues occupy a man's mind?

_____

_____

_____

6. How can men at church counter the many daily mental distractions that divert them from concentrating on spiritual growth?

_____

_____

Verse 15 continues, "Give thyself wholly to them." Literally Paul was saying, "Be these things; be absorbed, immersed in them."

7. With bills to pay, along with work and family commitments, how will being "absorbed and immersed" in spiritual character development be a blessing to a man? _____

_____

_____

Trailblazing Growth

The last part of verse 15 states, "That thy profiting may appear to all." The word "profiting" can also be translated "progress" and means "to cut," "to cut before," "to make headway, to forge ahead." It was used of a small army "cutting a path before" the larger army. It was used of pioneer work, that is, blazing a new trail, "to cut before."

Here's the point. Paul was saying, "You need to continually be experiencing pioneer advance in your spiritual life. New territories of uncharted, spiritual exploration await you. The growth taking place in your life ought to be visible."

8. In what uncharted spiritual territories do men at church need to make an observable "pioneer advance"? _____

_____

_____

9. Let's put it another way: What do children and teens need to see men at church doing?_____

_____

_____

Not doing? _____

_____

"Forward Ho!"

A look at the larger context of 1 Timothy 4:15 reveals that men at church need to be continually, observably making pioneer advances in three critical areas.

First, men at church need to make continual, observable advances in doctrinal discernment (1 Timothy 4:1–6).

10. Read 1 Timothy 4:1–6. How do we see in today's world some of the doctrinal errors that Paul wrote about in his day?

_____

_____

Be aware of these features of doctrinal deviation:
- It spreads like a cancer (2 Timothy 2:17).
- Its power is that of deceit and seduction (2 Timothy 3:13).
- It leads people away from God (2 Timothy 2:16).

11. Consider this: Your pastor has just resigned to take another ministry, and *you* are on the pulpit committee! How will your growth

in doctrinal discernment affect your effort as you look at pastoral candidates? What kind of factors will you be interested in?

_____

_____

_____

_____

_____

Second, men at church need to make continual, observable advances in godliness (1 Timothy 4:7–11).

Men and sports. It's like apple pie and ice cream; they just go together! Men admire a good athlete, because they understand the commitment and work ethic that is needed to achieve athletic excellence. Interestingly, Paul applied athletic imagery to our need to grow in godliness because many of the principles apply in both areas.

12. What does a man have to do to get into shape?

_____

_____

13. List various benefits of physical exercise.

- _____

- _____

- _____

- _____

14. How do the methods and benefits of physical discipline apply to the methods and benefits of spiritual discipline, or godliness (1 Timothy 4:7, 8)? _____

_____

_____

The word "godliness" in 1 Timothy 4:7 points to a visible contrast between false teachers, false doctrine, and *wrong* conduct, and true teachers, true doctrine, and *right* conduct. In short a godly man will practice what he preaches both inside and outside the church! (For additional study, note the other occurrences of the word "godliness" in the Pastoral Epistles: 1 Timothy 2:2; 3:16; 6:3, 5, 6, 11; 2 Timothy 3:5; Titus 1:1; 2:12.)

Third, men at church need to make continual, observable advances as examples (1 Timothy 4:12–16).

First Timothy 4:12 reads, "Be thou an example of the believers." The word "example" comes from a root word that means "to strike a blow or form something by an impression." It speaks of "a visible impression . . . a copy, image, pattern, model."

15. In light of this meaning of "example," what does being an example imply? _____

_____

16. Verse 12 reveals six key areas of spiritual growth. How can men make "pioneer advances" in each of them in their behavior at church?

• Speech _____

• Conduct _____

• Love _____

• Spirit_____

• Faith _____

• Purity _____

How old are you? How long have you been a member of your church? Whether you are young or more seasoned in years, the exciting thing about growth in Christ is that there are no age stipulations! Pray that God will use in your life this challenge of learning and growing as a man at church. Pray that the fruit of your growth would not be hidden but would be obvious and a delightful benefit to others!

5

MEN AT CHURCH ...

DON'T MAKE EXCUSES

This study will encourage you to value authentic commitment at church.

I N THE PASTORAL EPISTLES the apostle Paul intended to shore up Timothy, Titus, and their flocks in the essentials of authentic commitment to Christ. Paul wanted all his followers, not just himself, to finish well (2 Timothy 4:7). Yet he knew that the single-lane highway to ending well is heavily marked with attractive billboards that advertise enticing excuses to exit this "narrow road." In the opinion of many, this narrow road is simply too hard to travel (Matthew 7:13, 14; 2 Timothy 4:10).

Of all generations, ours is well acquainted with excuses. Whether it relates to a committed crime, a failed responsibility, or a declined opportunity, as a society we allow the excuses to ooze easily from our lips. We have a culture of excuse making. But as we learn from Paul, maturing men at church strive to *not* make excuses when it comes to the various aspects of living out true spirituality.

1. What does it mean to make an excuse?_____

_____

The *American Heritage Dictionary* defines it this way: "To apologize for, to seek to remove the blame from, to serve as a justification for, and to free from an obligation or duty."

"I can't do that *because* . . ."

2. Share some of the classic excuses you have heard men make at church about the following areas; record your answers.

• Involvement _____

_____

• Spiritual qualification for service _____

_____

• Faithful attendance to the services _____

_____

• Financial stewardship _____

_____

• Witnessing _____

_____

"Yes, I understand what you're saying, but have you ever thought . . ."

3. Review the list of excuses you compiled, and, on another sheet of paper, answer the following question for each one: A man just

made this excuse; how can you winsomely encourage him toward a Biblical alternative?

A Drive down Commitment Lane

Let's take a little trip through the Pastoral Epistles and view the scenery of authentic commitment as it is taught and illustrated throughout these books.

1 Timothy

Men at church don't make excuses about . . .

- Service (1:12)
- Their language (1:13)
- Their temper (1:13)
- Praying (2:1–3, 8)
- Character deficiencies (3:2–13)
- Family duties (3:4, 5, 11, 12)
- Doctrinal ignorance (4:1–5); can you spot a counterfeit?
- Quitting because of hurt feelings (4:10)
- Inexperience (4:12)
- Not reading the Bible (4:13)
- A lack of involvement (4:14)
- Not working (5:8)
- Not caring for family (5:16)
- Why they don't adequately compensate their pastor (5:17, 18)
- Showing favoritism (5:21)
- Moral purity (5:22)
- Their lack of a positive testimony at work (6:1, 2)
- Their lack of contentment (6:6)
- Greed (6:10)
- Their lack of spiritual effort (6:11, 12)
- The use of their resources (6:18)

Review the list from 1 Timothy and reflect on these questions.

4. In what areas do you find yourself prone to make excuses?

_____

_____

5. Why? _____

_____

6. Read the verse(s) that pertain to your need. Determine how the Biblical truth will help you be committed to the Lord in the area of your need. _____

_____

_____

2 Timothy

Men at church don't make excuses about . . .
- Fearing failure (1:7)
- Their testimony for Christ (1:8, 12)
- Spiritually drifting (1:13–15)
- Not having time to serve (1:17, 18)
- Their lack of strength (2:1); that is, the "I can't" syndrome
- Not being involved in other men's spiritual growth (2:2)
- Things being "too hard" (2:3–9)
- Giving up on people (2:10)
- Not having a basic knowledge of the Bible (2:15)
- Tolerating sin (2:19–22)
- Not fellowshipping with other believers (2:22)
- Impatience with people (2:24–26)
- Being less than a positive example (3:10, 11)
- Quitting (3:14)
- Biblical ignorance (3:15)
- Needing more than the Bible to solve life's dilemmas (3:16, 17)

- Backing away from people who are wrong (4:2–4)
- Not witnessing (4:5)
- Wanting to wait for Heaven (4:8); or "Please, Lord, let me get married *before* the Rapture!"
- Loving the things of the world (4:10)
- Giving up on people who have disappointed them (4:11)
- Having a vengeful spirit (4:14–16)
- Despairing in difficult circumstances (4:17, 18)

Review the list from 2 Timothy and reflect on these questions.

7. What areas do you find yourself prone to make excuses?

   _____

   _____

8. Why? _____

   _____

   _____

9. Read the verse(s) that pertain to your need. Determine how the Biblical truth will help you be committed to the Lord in your particular area of need. _____

   _____

   _____

Titus

Men at church don't make excuses about . . .

- A lack of personal and spiritual character (1:5–9)
- Being insubordinate (1:10); or "I'm just stubborn . . . that's the way I am!"
- A lack of spiritual maturity at an older age (2:2)
- Low expectations for young men (2:6–8)
- A lack of personal holiness (2:12)

- Not longing for Heaven (2:13, 14)
- Delayed obedience (3:1)
- Speaking evil about others (3:2)
- Holding on to the old life (3:3)
- Failure to deal with a divisive person in the church (3:10, 11)
- Not serving (3:14)

Review the list from Titus and reflect on these questions.

10. In what areas do you find yourself prone to make excuses?

_____

_____

11. Why? _____

_____

12. Read the verse(s) that pertain to your need. Determine how the Biblical truth will help you be committed to the Lord in your area of need. _____

_____

Prison. It's the last place from which you'd expect to get a letter of encouragement! Yet that is exactly the place from which Paul wrote the letters to Timothy and Titus. In light of his extremely difficult surroundings and circumstances, Paul could have made excuses, but you won't find any. Why? Because having been gripped by grace, Paul learned that the life of authentic commitment brings lasting blessing and joy. God is trustworthy, and Paul's experience of faith was worth whatever it cost him. The same is true today. Pray that you would find yourself saying yes to God more often in a renewed desire to practice real commitment as a godly man at church.

6

MEN AT CHURCH...

ARE TEAM PLAYERS

This study will teach you the importance of being a team player.

I WAS IN THE sixth grade and on the Yankees. Not the New York Yankees, but the Hamilton Township YMCA Yankees—a slight difference. It was the last game of the season, and we were facing the lowly Tigers, the team with the worst record. The smell of a sure victory was in the air. Strangely though, as things can go in sports, it came to the last inning, last ups, and we were behind. There were two outs, and I was up to bat. With mounting nervousness and wishing that somehow I could escape the spotlight of the moment, I struggled to a full count and struck out. We lost. The game was over, and the season was history.

I was absolutely humiliated. With head down, walking slowly away from home plate, I was quickly surrounded by my teammates, who proceeded to add insult to injury and pummel me with their ball gloves! Riding home in the car, I cried.

It is one thing to fail as a member of a team. It is another thing to fail and then be mistreated by those who you hoped would understand, help, and encourage.

Ground Rules

In 1 Timothy 3:1–13 Paul instructed Timothy in the details of God's criteria for leadership in the church. While these standards are specifically for pastors and deacons, they are lifestyle standards for *all* of God's people. The text is teaching that all pastors and deacons *must* have these character traits. However, *all* believers are to learn and incorporate them more and more.

This lesson will specifically focus on what we can learn from the criteria for a deacon. Yet its application is for *all* men who are on the roster of God's team at church!

God's Criteria for Team Players

The men on God's team know their position
(1 Timothy 3:8, "deacons").

A good athlete knows his position well and may have the ability to play multiple positions. Interestingly, this word translated "deacon" and other related words appear approximately one hundred times in the New Testament. In only two of these occurrences is it translated "deacon," an official helping capacity in the church: here in 1 Timothy 3:8 and in Philippians 1:1. The word means "service" and refers to the performance of any variety of tasks including seemingly menial ones, such as waiting on tables.

What's the point? Godly men at church know their position and play it well. They are servants and are willing to do whatever is needed to help the team!

1. A team player knows that when he does his job in his position, the entire team is helped. Look up Romans 12:6–13 and 1 Corinthians 16:15 and explain the benefits for your church when men "play" these positions of service.

_____

_____

_____

Many Christians believe that Acts 6:1–6 records the establishment of the office of deacon. The nature of this office is "service," but it is important to note that the office was established to stop the murmuring and complaining that was dividing the church (v. 1).

2. What needed "positions" in the church can men take when the unity of the team is threatened by complaining and murmuring?

_____

_____

_____

Team players wear their game face (1 Timothy 3:8, "grave").

3. When we refer to an athlete and say, "He's got his game face on," what do we mean? _____

_____

_____

The word "grave" means "reverent, serious, and stately." It could be translated "men of dignity" and indicates that those characterized as "grave" have a majestic quality of character. The athlete who is wearing his game face is not on the field watching planes fly overhead or picking dandelions. Rather, he is intense and serious about winning. Likewise, team players at church are spiritually tuned in to what is going on at church. While they are not cold and joyless, they are se-rious about what it means to follow God's game plan.

**Team players don't take verbal shots at their teammates
(1 Timothy 3:8, "not doubletongued").**

4. Give an example of teammates taking verbal shots at each other in
   sports? _____

   _____

   _____

   _____

5. Give an example of how verbal shots take place at church.

   _____

   _____

On a well-coached team, difficulties are discussed in closed-door meetings within the locker-room walls. What is said inside stays in-side. Likewise at church, godly men don't gossip.

**Team players stay away from "performance enhancers"
(1 Timothy 3:8, "not given to much wine").**

Athletes are tempted with both "on-field" (e.g., steroids) and "off-field" (e.g., drugs and alcohol) performance enhancers. However, in the end, the consequences can be deadly.

6. Sports trivia question: Recount the story of performance enhanc-ers in the life of football player Lyle Alzado of the Oakland Raid-ers. _____

   _____

   _____

The word "given" means "addicted to," or "to turn one's mind to." It refers to the fact that the team player is not to be preoccupied with drink or to allow it to influence his life.

7. Why is alcohol such an attraction for men, and what are its dangers? _____

_____

_____

Team players play for the love of the game (1 Timothy 3:8, "not greedy of filthy lucre").

While inflated salaries are a source of contention in professional sports, a true athlete is not motivated by greed. Likewise, men at church do not have any ulterior motives for service other than a genuine love for the Lord and the desire to please Him!

8. What ulterior motives might men have for involvement at church? _____

_____

_____

Team players have a deep appreciation for the integrity of the game (1 Timothy 3:9, "holding the mystery of the faith in a pure conscience").

The game of golf is built upon the foundation of integrity. There are rules to follow even when no one else knows you violated them. Likewise, the standard of faith and practice for men at church is the content of Biblical revelation. Men at church know that "all things are naked and opened unto the eyes of him with whom we have to do" (Hebrews 4:13). Consequently, by means of a life of obedience they enjoy the freedom and blessing of a clear conscience.

9. What are the blessings of knowing you are living in obedience to the Scriptures? _____

_____

_____

Team players learn the lessons of the rookie season (1 Timothy 3:10, "And let these also first be proved; then let them . . .").

10. What are the characteristics of a rookie? _____

_____

_____

_____

Rookies are never captains. They need experience. A rookie might have raw talent, but it needs to be tempered and tutored by veterans. A veteran understands the long haul of the season and has learned that you don't quit when you have a bad game. He understands what it takes to achieve real victory.

11. How can veteran believers in your church encourage the rookies (new believers)? _____

_____

_____

Team players accept the responsibility of being a role model (1 Timothy 3:10, "being found blameless").

"I am not a role model!" Do you remember this disclaimer by Charles Barkley? There was a day when professional athletes accepted this badge of honor in light of their privileged position. However, in a day when character means nothing and athletic competency is the only thing, we will continue to see the Charles Barkleys rise to stardom in the eyes of men and women. A real man who is learning and growing in godliness shoulders the responsibility of being a role model. "Blameless" does not mean "perfect." It simply means that your life is such that you would not have a panic attack if "60 Minutes" showed up on your doorstep to do an exposé on the closets of your life.

12. What is the value to the church when men are authentic role

models of godliness? _____

_____

_____

Team players keep their "off-field life" in order (1 Timothy 3:11–13, "Even so must their wives be . . ."; ". . . [they must] be the husbands of one wife").

Team players keep their homelife in order so that it won't distract the team. Men at church take their marital vows seriously. They work hard at being a one-woman man in both thought and action. They don't play around with pornography, thinking it will spice up their love life, because they understand that women view intimacy as more than a physical act.

13. What are some specific things men can do to safeguard their marriages? _____

_____

_____

Team players support the coach (1 Timothy 5:17, "Let the elders that rule well be counted worthy of double honour, especially they who labour in the word and doctrine").

14. What do players appreciate in a coach? _____

_____

_____

15. What creative things can men do to show respect and appreciation for their pastor? _____

_____

_____

_____

The Losers. One of the men in my church used to play for a softball team with that name. It was the first thing opposing teams saw on the players' T-shirts, and it brought jibes and jokes. That was until the game began. The opposing teams did not know, until it was too late, that the Losers were former all-star athletes and would consistently mop up the field with the competition!

The world often sees men at church as losers. "For the preaching of the cross is to them that perish foolishness; but unto us [who] are saved it is the power of God" (1 Corinthians 1:18). What the world does not realize is that "we are more than conquerors through him that loved us" (Romans 8:37)! Men at church are winners when they encourage that teammate who struck out and when they work hard on the fundamentals of godly living. Team players are not self-willed, full of pride, antagonistic, and critical of others. Pray that God would make you into a productive team player for His glory!

7

MEN AT CHURCH . . .

DEAL WITH DIFFERENCES

This lesson will equip you with needed skill in resolving problems with people.

D IFFERENCES ARE AS old as Cain and Abel. Even at the outset of New Testament church life, differences erupted (Acts 6:1). Unfortunately, both New Testament evidence and church history testify that this volcano continues to be active throughout the church worldwide. Because all of us are still fixed to our unredeemed flesh, differences in the life of the church will be a reality until Heaven is our home. Until then, the issue for us men is to deal with differences as God would have us.

"Them's Fight'n Words!"
In the days of the early church, certain situations created more

heat than light. Consequently, a lot of "fight'n words" were flying around! Learning how Paul instructed Timothy and Titus to deal with such situations will serve us well in dealing with our differences today.

1. What do we mean when we say we have a difference with someone? _____

_____

The *American Heritage Dictionary* states that to have a "difference" means "to be of a different opinion, to disagree, to quarrel, to dispute; the cause of a disagreement or controversy." Though it would be nice to say differences do not occur among believers, the fact remains that even good men can have differences at church.

The Church at War

Note the following truths about serving the Lord:

• Biblical church life *demands* a battlefield mindset (1 Timothy 1:18: "warfare," *strateia*, used of spiritual conflict).

• Fighting is *supposed* to happen in church (1 Timothy 6:12: "fight," *agon*, from which we get "agonize, conflict, fight").

• *Conflict* is the hallmark of our spiritual journey (2 Timothy 4:7: "fought . . . fight," *agonizomai*, "to contend, to strive as in a contest for a prize, straining every nerve to obtain the object").

Here's the dilemma: while we want to avoid harmful friction in the church, these Scripture passages show us that fighting *is* to take place in the church.

But here's the problem: in our church life we men often battle the wrong enemy! All too many churches are devastated because men who can't get along are tossing grenades into fellow soldiers' tents.

Throwing Dirt

Most men don't get squeamish with a little dirt. In fact for many men, dirt under the fingernails is a stylish accessory with jeans and a flannel shirt. Dirt because of hard work is one thing. Dirt in church work is quite another. Let's look at some of the common areas where men sometimes "throw dirt" in church.

Projects

2. You are one of the trustees. Your church needs to replace the orange carpet in the sanctuary. What are the steps you will take to work through this decision in a manner that pleases God and avoids friction with three of the committee members who originally chose the carpet in 1970? _____

_____

_____

_____

Policies

3. How can the area of church policies be a real hot potato and burn a church? _____

_____

_____

_____

4. What safeguards need to be in place in a legitimate desire to do things "decently and in order" (1 Corinthians 14:40) yet keep a ministry focused on Christ? _____

_____

_____

Politics

5. Fred and Francine are career missionaries, and your ministry is their honored sending church. Your church has supported them for twenty years. You are a new member on the missions commit-

tee. Recently you discovered that your church hasn't received one
report from them in the past eight years. How would you address
this issue? Oh, by the way, Francine is the daughter of the chair-
man of the board of deacons. _____

_____

_____

_____

Personalities

Someone has said, "If it weren't for the people, the ministry
wouldn't be too bad!"

6. You are the Devil. What would you do to wreak havoc in the
   church, using the various personalities that make up a church?

   _____

   _____

   _____

When Differences Divide

Sometimes the issues that might create tension among men at
church are necessary; for example, if someone were teaching wrong
doctrine. At other times unfortunate personality conflicts and a variety of other situations take place. Paul made the point to Timothy
and Titus to *deal with* a situation—whatever the cause. Sweeping it
under the rug would not work.

Let's look at a sampling of the issues that Paul addressed in each
of the Pastoral Epistles—issues that were hurting the church and that
involved both men and women.

Look up the following references and answer questions 7–9 about
each one. (Use another sheet of paper or a blank page in this book.)

1 Timothy	2 Timothy	Titus
5:13	2:14–16	2:3
5:19	2:23–26	3:2
6:4	4:3	3:9
6:20, 21	4:14, 15	3:10, 11

7. What does the passage say? _____

_____

_____

8. How could this issue, or these issues, creep into your church and create harmful division? _____

_____

_____

9. What godly responses to each situation would bring about reconciliation and unity? _____

_____

_____

How to Avoid Division from Differences

We can avoid letting differences cause divisions if we observe six principles.

• **Don't be distracted with nonessentials (2 Timothy 2:4).**

10. What things do men need to do at church to keep from getting tangled up in issues that don't matter? _____

_____

_____

- **Don't have a private agenda (2 Timothy 2:4).**
11. What do private agendas look like in a church, and how will understanding 2 Timothy 2:4 minimize this problem?

_____

_____

_____

_____

- **Pray a lot (1 Timothy 2:1).**
12. How does prayer safeguard relationships with authority figures whom God places in our lives but with whom we might differ?

_____

_____

- **Watch the pride factor (1 Timothy 6:1–4).**
13. How will the sin of pride in men hinder resolving a difference?

_____

_____

- **Be winsome with your words (2 Timothy 2:24–26).**
14. From this text, describe the traits of a wise man who works effectively with problem people. _____

_____

_____

- **Refuse to speak evil of another (Titus 3:2).**
15. How does this verse relate to the atmosphere of business meetings in your church? _____

_____

16. Testimony check: Divide Titus 3:2 in half at the word "but." Which half is your reputation? Do you speak evil of others; are you a brawler (v. 2a)? Or are you gentle and meek (v. 2b)? Check your testimony: (v. 2a) _____ or (v. 2b) _____

Do you need to resolve a difference with someone right now? God's way is not to wish away the problem or to sweep it under the rug. Too many churches suffer because of the deterioration that results when men do that. Most often the biggest problem is our pride (including fear that we could be wrong). Pray that God would equip you with the spiritual skills needed to be a peacemaker in problems; then humble yourself and do it.

8

MEN AT CHURCH . . .

STICK IT OUT

This lesson will teach you the lifelong benefit of endurance.

S TICK IT OUT! Come on . . . keep going . . . you can do it!" These are words of encouragement men hear and use in the arena of competition. "Stick it out" is a slang expression that means "to persist, endure, persevere, to remain firm, determined, resolute, to remain loyal or faithful." "Stick it out" encapsulates the desire to finish strong and well. Likewise, it challenges men in the truth that perseverance is essential if we are serious about being a "marathon model" of living for the Lord.

Men Stoppers 101

"Quitters never win and winners never quit." He did not coin the phrase, but my dad spoke as if he owned the copyright on it. Not only did I hear it often as a boy and teen, but I saw it lived out by my dad at church. Through thick and thin he stuck it out and blazed a legacy of faithfulness for me to follow. To this point in my journey, I still don't know what it's like to quit, because my dad never showed me how.

Someone once said, "The test of your character is what it takes to stop you." As we have already studied, even men who love God in a local church aren't exempt from the possibility of difficulties. It is critical to understand that trials have stopping power only to the degree that we let them.

Let's look at some of the common issues that will hit men head-on and that, for some of those men, may stop them in their spiritual tracks.

Troubles (with problems) can stop a man in his tracks.

1. Describe the problems you have witnessed men struggle with that ultimately became their excuse to turn from the Lord.

   _____

   _____

   _____

   _____

Turmoil (with people) can stop a man in his tracks.

2. What is it about experiencing turmoil with people that makes it easy for men to conclude that working through a problem is just too difficult? _____

   _____

   _____

   _____

   _____

Timidity (with predicaments) can stop a man in his tracks.

3. How can fear be a factor in hindering men from making spiritual progress? _____

_____

_____

Time (with priorities) can stop a man in his tracks.

4. How is it possible for men to crowd their lives with so many *good* things that the *best* things get crowded out? _____

_____

_____

Temptation (with private sins) can stop a man in his tracks.

5. What are the subtle but observable spiritual evidences that signal a struggle with secret sin? _____

_____

_____

Teaching (with Biblical principles) can stop a man in his tracks.

6. What Biblical teachings can be a turnoff to men who have yet to learn the blessings of surrendering their lives to the authority of the Scriptures? _____

_____

_____

Tithing (the problem of the purse) can stop a man in his tracks.

7. Think about all you have learned about putting Christ first in your finances. How would you encourage a new believer with what you have learned? _____

_____

Men at Church "Stick It Out" Because . . .

Let's discover the underlying spiritual character traits that sustain men who purposely live for the long haul.

They accept the difficulties involved in spiritual warfare (2 Timothy 2:3).

8. Why does a country need soldiers? _____

_____

_____

9. In the heat of battle, what are soldiers vulnerable to? _____

_____

_____

Warfare can cause wounds. In particular, men need to watch out for the land mines of "people 'plosions." These blowups are not so much antagonistic attacks against you as they are failure by others. "People 'plosions" are those discouraging experiences when the people you look up to or count on fall apart because of hardship or sin.

10. Read 2 Timothy 1:15 and 4:10. Describe what occurred in each verse and how similar difficulties can happen today. _____

_____

_____

_____

_____

_____

_____

The key to not caving in and quitting when hit by the shrapnel of disappointment with people is to "endure" (2 Timothy 2:3). The word here means "to suffer misfortune, trouble, toil, exertion, enduring suffering." It follows an extended context of situations that can occur in the messy arena of people work (1:15—2:3). Men who endure and survive the difficulties of authentic discipleship are men who are spiritually thick-skinned. They are not easily offended, moody, or constantly paranoid with incessant thoughts about themselves. They are mature men who can persevere even with an emotional hole blown through their heart, because they accept the difficulties involved in spiritual warfare.

Men who endure know what it takes to see lost people rescued (2 Timothy 2:10).

Paul was willing to "suffer trouble" and even false accusation because of his confidence in the awesome power of the Word of God to liberate men's lives (2 Timothy 2:9). In light of that truth, he resolved, "Therefore I endure all things for the elect's sakes, that they may also obtain the salvation which is in Christ Jesus" (v. 10). Paul knew that the key to effectiveness in reaching people is not to give up, but to endure. This word means "to stay in a place, to hold out, to stand fast, to stay still, to remain."

11. Carefully review the meanings of the word translated "endure." How are these concepts essential in reaching lost people for Christ? _____

_____

_____

Men who endure comprehend the value of future reward and the high cost of potential denial (2 Timothy 2:12).

Second Timothy 2:12 makes the cost of confessing Christ very high ("if we suffer") and thereby tests one's true faith. Men at church comprehend the brevity of life in contrast to the big picture of eternity ("we shall also reign with him"). Therefore they make decisions on the basis of eternal value, not temporary gain.

12. Name some tough decisions that men at church can make during this life that they will never regret for all eternity. _____

_____

_____

Men who endure are committed to learning sound doctrine while others are not (2 Timothy 4:3).

Biblically grounded men at church understand that in their current culture and in a multiplicity of ways there is a growing distain for doctrine. Paul stated it in a way that still rings true today: there are those who will "not endure" sound doctrine. Here the word "endure" means "to receive, take up, and bear." The question is, What kind of doctrine was Paul referring to? A look at verse 2 reveals that the kind of doctrine men will not "take up and receive" brings three things to the table: conviction ("reprove"), correction ("rebuke"), and compulsion to change ("exhort"). I call this the doctrine of "mirror-ology": when you look into a mirror, you can't escape the facts!

13. What Biblical teaching have you learned that, when you first held its truth in front of your face, brought conviction and correction and compelled you to change? _____

_____

_____

Men who endure desire the delight of finishing well (2 Timothy 4:5).

Someone has said, "Too many men want the thrill of feeling right without the inconvenience of being right."

14. What four commands of 1 Timothy 4:5 will help men at church "be right" and persevere to the end?

• _____

• _____

- _____
- _____

15. Describe how each command will contribute to a man's ultimate goal of finishing strong and finishing well. _____

_____

_____

_____

_____

_____

_____

_____

Men at church persevere. They stick it out through thick and thin. They make daily decisions that will minimize regret and maximize lasting joy. One hymnwriter said it this way: "It will be worth it all when we see Jesus." And as another writer put it, "God will not look you over for medals, degrees, or diplomas, but for scars." At times you will be battle weary and scarred; but pray that at the end of your spiritual journey, you, like Paul, will victoriously declare, "I have finished my course, I have kept the faith!"

WRAP IT UP

1. Rate your application of these Bible truths of what men at church are to be, with 5 being the highest.

Men are to attend church regularly.

      1   2   3   4   5

Men are to lead and serve at church according to God's directions, not their own.

      1   2   3   4   5

Men are excited about God's continuing grace in their lives.

      1   2   3   4   5

Men are growing and changing, not satisfied with the status quo in themselves.

      1   2   3   4   5

Men do not excuse the sin in their lives; they deal with (confess, repent, change) sin.

      1   2   3   4   5

Men are "more than conquerors" through Jesus Christ.

      1   2   3   4   5

Men fight sin and falsehood, not one another.

      1   2   3   4   5

Men "finish [their] course"; they don't quit somewhere along the way.

      1   2   3   4   5

2. Identify a way in which you are a positive role model at church. Write out a plan for continuing strong (and even growing) in that area. _____

_____

_____

_____

_____

3. Write out a plan for encouraging another man in this area.

_____

_____

_____

_____

4. Identify your three greatest struggles when it comes to you and church. Write out a game plan for victory. _____

_____

_____

_____

_____

_____

_____

_____

_____